Go Green!

Written by Dan White

Contents

Planet Earth

This is what Planet Earth looks like from far away. It is stunning!

We need to look after it and we can all help in different ways.

Rubbish

People get new things all the time. Many of the things end up in landfill.

Landfills are big piles of rubbish.

The factories that make these things pump out harmful fumes too.

Problem Plastic

When you throw away plastic, do you think it just vanishes? Sadly, plastic often ends up in the sea.

Animals can mistake it for food and eat it. This makes them very ill.

Think green!
Do not litter! Put any rubbish in a bin or use it again.

Make a toy!

Terrific Trees

Trees are important. Lots of animals live in forests. Trees also clean the air for us.

The number of trees on Earth is getting smaller every year. People cut them down for wood or to clear land for farming.

Think green!
When trees are cut down, new ones
can be planted. However, it takes
years for trees to grow, so we must
protect forests too.

Smelly Smog

Cars pump out fumes that fill the air.

Air that is full of fumes is called smog.

Cars make gases that trap the Sun's heat. This makes it hotter on Earth.

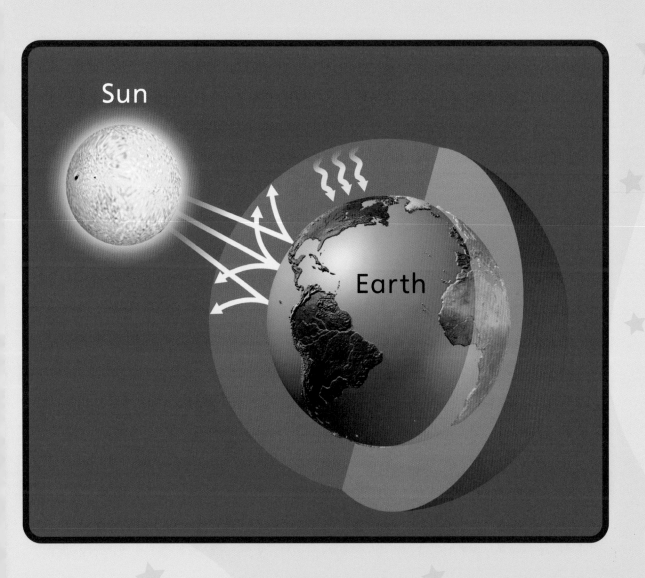

Think green!
Use your feet or ride a bike whenever you can. Use public transport, where lots of people travel together.

There is a lot to do ... but if we all think green, we can make things better!

Index